the eighth day of the week

MAREK HLASKO

the eighth day of the week

TRANSLATED FROM THE POLISH

BY NORBERT GUTERMAN

GREENWOOD PRESS, PUBLISHERS
WESTPORT, CONNECTICUT

Library of Congress Cataloging in Publication Data

Hłasko, Marek.
  The eighth day of the week.

  Translation of Ósmy dzień tygodnia.
  Reprint of the 1st ed. published by Dutton, New York.
  I. Title.
[PZ4.H678Ei4] [PG7158.H55]   891.8'5'37   74-27462
ISBN 0-8371-7896-7

Translated from the Polish ÓSMY DZIEŃ TYGODNIA

Copyright © 1958 by E. P. Dutton & Co., Inc.

Originally published in 1958 by E. P. Dutton & Co., Inc., New York

Reprinted with the permission of the publishers, E. P. Dutton and Company, Inc.

Reprinted in 1975 by Greenwood Press, a division of Williamhouse-Regency Inc.

Library of Congress Catalog Card Number 74-27462

ISBN 0-8371-7896-7

Printed in the United States of America

the eighth day of the week